ANYTHING & EVERYTHING

OTHER WORK IN ENGLISH BY MICHEL DELVILLE

POETRY

Third Body (Quale Press, 2009; translated by Gian Lombardo)

CRITICISM

~~Undoing~~ *Art,* with Mary Ann Caws (Quodlibet, 2016)

Crossroads Poetics: Text, Image, Music, Film & Beyond (Litteraria Pragensia, 2014)

Food, Poetry, and the Aesthetics of Consumption: Eating the Avant-Garde (Routledge, 2012)

Frank Zappa, Captain Beefheart and the Secret History of Maximalism, with Andrew Norris (Salt Publishing, 2005)

The American Prose Poem: Poetic Form and the Boundaries of Genre (University Press of Florida, 1998)

J. G. Ballard (Northcote House Publishers, 1998)

ANYTHING & EVERYTHING

PROSE POEMS & MICROESSAYS

MICHEL DELVILLE

TRANSLATED FROM THE FRENCH BY GIAN LOMBARDO

QUALE PRESS

This publication was funded by the Interuniversity Attraction Pole Programme initiated by the Belgian Science Policy Office (BELSPO-IAP-PAI 7/01).

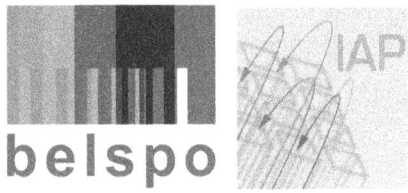

This book was originally published in Belgium as *Entre la poire et le fromage* © 2013 Michel Delville and Les Éditions de l'Entourloupe.

Translation © 2016 by Gian Lombardo

Cover photo by Elisabeth Waltregny © 2016, www.elisabethwaltregny.com

ISBN: 978-1-935835-19-6 trade paperback edition

LCCN: 2016948537

Quale Press
www.quale.com

Contents

Andres Serrano \ 3
Andy Warhol \ 4
Antonio Lobo Antunes \ 6
Saint Catherine of Siena \ 7
Damien Hirst \ 9
David Lynch \ 10
Don Van Vliet \ 11
Donatien Alphonse François de Sade \ 12
Erik Satie \ 14
Eugène Savitzkaya \ 15
Filippo Tommaso Marinetti \ 16
Francis Bacon \ 17
Francis Ponge \ 18
Franz Kafka \ 20
Georges Braque \ 22
Gertrude Stein \ 23
Herman Melville \ 25
James Joyce \ 26

Joris-Karl Huysmans \ 28
Joseph Cornell \ 29
Marcel Broodthaers \ 30
Marcel Duchamp \ 32
Marcel Proust \ 33
Max Ernst \ 35
Michel de Montaigne \ 36
Paul Claudel \ 38
Percy Bysshe Shelley \ 40
Peter Greenaway \ 41
Piero Manzoni \ 43
Salvador Dalí \45
Samuel Beckett \ 46
Steve Reich \ 48
Wayne Thiebaud \ 49
William Faulkner \ 51
Wim Delvoye \ 52
Wyndham Lewis \ 53

Notes \ 54

*Silk
Cap,
Ivory
Pecker,
Very black
Outfit,
Paul watches
The hutch,
Sticks
Tongue
At pear,
Prepares,
Conducts,
And dumps.*
—«Young Glutton,»
  Arthur Rimbaud

*Between the fruit course and cheese course,
when you can talk about
anything and everything.*

To Elisabeth, Romain and Louise

ANDRES SERRANO

If his name incites violence perpetrated on flesh, his work is far closer to the filthy preciousness of reliquaries. Sacred beauty of depravity, spritzing yellow bubbles and a cibachrome-orange tint. The sacrificial item's elsewhere, beyond grasp, rendered unconsumable and inconceivable. Even the jar containing the original configuration can't be conceived.

Andy Warhol

Why did he husband his faith after having promoted the canning of food? A child's eye surrendering to the stained glass windows of the Church of Saint Jean Chrysostome already sucks in solace. Sensuously sinking into their oblong shapes. Base senses overtake loftier, recharged by the bright colors of Byzantine frescos. A bundle of flesh, muscles and nerves on edge, he wanders around, sniffing, feeling his way, lunging at columns and licking dank walls. Afterward, he will forge the myth of his first baby steps relative to his restlessness at that instant. He will live solely in his exhalation, in his gaze, his desire to enjoy that image and to endlessly reproduce it so he can enjoy it over and over. The game's so clear he sees himself through it.

Back at the family homestead, he comes across a crucifix placed on a mantelpiece. This very familiar object opens floodgates to forthcoming troubles. Julia, daughter of the ocean, absent mother of mercy, ascends to a silent cloud swathed in blue. The kitten died (*Little Hester who left for pussy heaven*). A reproduction of the *Last Supper* by Leonardo da Vinci is slipped into the book of prayers, which will bring to a close the artist's candy pink period. After years of crazed retifism, rows of cans and bottles of Coke, celebrity portraits and road wrecks, surges an ecstasy crushed by a pain that rips through his gut. Surfacing unseen, the specter expands and contracts in the same pulse of adaptation. The slow and tiresome enumeration of the smallest details of the room summons the intricately woven part of his mind in which everything possible and everything unimaginable are intertwined. The moment vanishes, and we're left with joy upon awakening, in perfect harmony with everything around us.

Antonio Lobo Antunes

You who scaled peaks, where you experienced beauty and death made you stronger every day. There you lay prostrate, overcome, like a rat. Your trembling hands, your arms and legs so pale, wrenched in some kind of spasm. You try to crawl a bit further, but your body no longer belongs to you, you no longer feel your thighs, and your clothes hang heavy with fresh blood. Your handsome blue eyes open wide, your pupils dilate, your jaws clench. There's a metallic aftertaste in your throat. Your tongue is parched and scorched. Your unscathed intelligence listens for diagnoses. Every word, every line you will write for that child's face ashen against the light. You would whisper something to him, but you fall asleep without knowing what's new, what future to speak and speak again.

Saint Catherine of Siena

Daughter of a cloth dyer, Catherine is the twenty-third child of a cantankerous middle-class woman who gave up breastfeeding her twin sister, hoping that at least one of them would thrive. Weaning occurs very early, and the nipple is immediately coated with the bitter juice of aloe at the start of the next pregnancy. A part of the scrawny little girl dies with her own twin's extinction and she decides never to marry. Future patron of anorexic body artists, she shuns all sustenance except for a crust of bread and some lumps of oatmeal. Quenching her thirst in the blood and sweat of the crucified, satiated with the good and holy desire for the salvation of souls, she's reborn from the openings in the flesh of torture victims. She knows that life resides within those wounds and glimpses her salvation in an intuitive vision of the revolutionary vocation of the water fast. Later on, Catherine cuts her hair, renounces every kind of nourishment and officially launches her political career. She will write many dialogs and nearly four hundred letters addressed to citizens, priests, prelates and the pope. One day, her abused flesh will peel away from its skeleton, as if to embody the vanity of all this turmoil, all those fears that torment us. Our time is short, run without carelessness and without ignorance. The exquisite agony of holy desire ends with life.

In a painting by Giovanni di Paolo she holds a book in her left hand and in the other a lily stalk. Her head is tilted at a slight angle, bathed in gold, and as pale as the veil that envelops her. Her long emaciated fingers seem as fragile as crystal. Her sallow eyes are tired but haven't given up, her pupils shrunken but not empty. Her gaze retains a keenness that breaks beyond the panel's confines, carrying the young woman beyond common sensation. The starched folds of her white dress and her dark cloak bestow a more literal meaning to the work, something more solid, and which banishes any ordinary feelings of sadness and pity. Two sickly cherubs flank the saint. Squished onto the wooden panel, their ordinariness contrasts with the striking strangeness of this figure simultaneously so specific and so indeterminant.

Damien Hirst

A drop of water can encompass a room.
Ping-pong balls floating on red liquid.
A garbage-strewn path.
Colorless light.

Another prick in the mall.

David Lynch

An odd animal stands upright on its hind legs blocking the opening to the clearing. Behind him, a beam of light caroms off the ground, revealing a human figure that the patchy fog partially obscures. The stranger immediately disappears and the expanse of the sky lights up in a brilliant exercise of sultry Italian seduction. Animals take off down the creek, issuing sharp crics, amazed and frightened by this extraordinary turnabout. The child, he remains there, drawn to what feels like a gift from heaven. He then notices rows of tiny houses all gray and funereal, made indistinct by damp air and from which escape some snatches of sentences spoken in an inverted language. Behind the curtain of leaves he foretells a future that is absolutely impossible to fathom. He lowers one knee to the ground and picks a small handful of raspberries that he swallows hungrily. The houses fall silent and fade away. Lying on the earth, he decides to be fully present and never grounds for dream and transformation.

Don Van Vliet

A carp disguised as a trout. The man in the conical hat assumes the look of such a mask with undetermined sex unchained by worlds. Sight jumbled, birdbrained, swollen with silence. To trick those who think evading a universe teeming with flesh, with fiber and mucous membranes, with sex, birth and death. A well-known pornographer bought the mask and preserves that relic. *Pig Erases a Statue in Passing*. All this not worth moonlight in Vermont.

DONATIEN ALPHONSE FRANÇOIS DE SADE

Here, everything is permitted save remorse and lack of discipline, relentlessly dissolving and regurgitating as quickly as possible. The regime is strict — it requires beatings, shocks, probings and the most violent emetics. The calculating animal protects itself from the pitfalls of self-analysis, avoids familiar figures of revolutionary utopia, seizes the body, hoping to fashion a definitive condition for bourgeois dogma and repressive neoliberalist discourse. His own narrative swallowed whole by the laws of nature, he veers from understanding the ultimate consequences of a catatonic state when plunged into nocturnal visions, in the instant that separates life from death, enjoyment from satisfaction.

On an impeccably set table, a pale and voluptuous body is exposed to view. She opens her eyes and notices cracks and ridges of the ceiling compose a compulsory litany. Gestures are devoted to the annihilation of the victim and to the anticipated commemoration of the flood of her screams. The non-subject's suffering must be observed, exacerbated and shared. What do we know, exactly, of desire? Who's its architect? Does fantasy neutralize memory or, on the other hand, crack it open into infinity? To fear comparisons and expect the worst.

Erik Satie

Unlike devotees of Chef Greenaway, who devour black food concocted as an antidote against the fear of death, Satie claims to dine exclusively on white food: eggs, sugar, ground bones, fat from dead animals, veal, salt, coconut, chicken cooked in floured water, fruit mold, rice, turnips, camphor pudding, pasta, cheese (white), cotton salad and certain fish (without skin).

Eugène Savitzkaya

Contemplate stars run aground on silty prose, magnificent imprecision. A prose representing the intimacy of being in touch with thought itself. Fingers massage, sculpt and polish without possessing. A voice chews, sniffs, sings and chants in an attempt at close, almost prehensile, reading of objects. There is no threshold or conclusion to the motion of desire swallowing up the double body. Nothing can quench the thirst to know the tiniest details of the operation that governs peeling, chopping and placing a potato in boiling water. It's distinguished from a Ponge-ian approach by its concern for non-projection of the self and its contempt for anthropomorphism. It exits the world to evangelize its continuity, kindles in us what's unfinished, revives the forces of the future, strokes the heady structures of memory. Stick out a rough tongue, skin tensed and mind stupefied. Thoughts drink by listening to a story that lends itself to silent reading, which, since Ambrose of Milan, places greater emphasis on the interjection of intense and discrete feelings. Thus reigns order and chaos in Mad Jizm City, as in its many gardens, plots and other arable land. Seek but never find a similar non-beginning. Savor the heights of simplicity.

Filippo Tommaso Marinetti

Vegetarian cubist square. An initial splash followed by ultranationalist flirtations. Subtle nuances of antimatter. Abolition of mass and volume. Flattening of forms. Mannerisms of tactilism and polymorphic orality. Raw meat shredded by trumpet blasts. A taste for metal that sows death under the pretext of rekindling life. The terrorism of hopelessness. Developing a constant and progressive synthesis of dawning senses. Mixing competing and muddled flavors and colors, overstimulating nerves, throwing insides into upheaval, firing instincts. An abundance of greed, insatiable fighting regiments, preservative agents in a state of advanced hilarity, shifting into the realm of fight promotion, rank and file subsiding into a hyper-erotic world where every surface becomes pleated, where every wound is the source of delight and, better yet, antidote to boredom. To paint the interior walls of the stomach, slathered as they are with searing savors. Gobbling the world whole, with its stockpiles of rice, its panettone and stuffed Milanese hams. Then regurgitate multicolored bouquets. Freed words, exploded bloody body parts as in Adrianopolis. Destinies dismissed by the world's hygiene and the tyrany of innovation.

Francis Bacon

Clutter of chairs, oozing flesh subject to the most unlikely rumors. Half the paint on the front door has weathered off. Eyes wide with horror howl in silence. Hands are placed on the table and nervously explore its seams. The window cracked open lets in moisture from an afternoon rainshower, yellow and ocher tints. She steps forward and kisses the old man seated on his maroon easychair. A glass falls, breaks and resounds. Like a laugh. Wine flows under the table and slowly inches toward the door. The walls are pock-marked and light interferes with pores, causing discomfort arising from a disagreement between the duty of deception and the persistence of memory.

Francis Ponge

At the market, a vendor sells him some blue plums picked the day before. Back home, after having dumped them in a wicker basket lying in the kitchen, he moves them onto the exposed edge of the window sill. The next day only rain and dew roll off the thin coat of waxy dust adhering to their surfaces.

To peel an orange gives him dazzlements carried on the fullness of a strong and exaggerated gesture. Unlike Louis McNeice (*I peel and portion / A tangerine and spit the pips and feel / The drunkenness of things being various*), Ponge seems to know only the intoxication of words. Far from that, where everything is just heartbreak, possession and clinging desire, figures which will later give way to those of exchange, transmission and giving.

Franz Kafka

He places the pinnacle of professional fasting in the mid-19th century, a period when a show staged by the hunger artist brought in the bucks and monopolized the attention of whole communities. The auteur underscores the «wonder» with which the public — especially children — was transfixed at the sight of emaciated limbs and protruding bones of the body of the artist laid on straw.

His long, lean back pressed against the back of the chair, he said reading Milena's letters was like a sparrow pecking at crumbs. Uncommon thrill, overpowering pleasure in words made flesh.

GEORGES BRAQUE

Still Life with Pear (1939). Abolition of depth, starched pleats, exile from base senses. This painting impresses by its stiff line and lack of psychological closeness. The artist took care to tidy up the mess caused by slicing and eating the absent pear half. The fruit is ripe. I eat it and by consequence am no longer. Grape berries placed one beside the other are no longer grapes. They have become fruit. As for the gritty flesh of *Pyrus communis*, it will never rot in writing or through a canvas decomposing. It will withstand anyone talking about it, converting it into sound. Shouts, fits, thunder, earthquakes, tsunamis, falling meteorites. Expertise must meet the beauty tendered, without word-glut and without shame. And life to become a trifle less convincing for explorers of the unseen.

GERTRUDE STEIN

Monday: green beans and bowel cramps. Tuesday: cauliflower and spiritual exercises. Wednesday: flying contraptions, astral transport and cheese plate. Thursday: roast beef and free inquiry. Friday: sole *meunière* and exploitation of global resources. Saturday: chervil *velouté* and metaphysical licks. Sunday: ravioli with truffles and official hijinks. Monday: quiche Lorraine and postcolonial transactions. Tuesday: cucumber salad and an Electra complex. Wednesday: quince charlotte and euphemisms scaling Montmartre. Thursday: roasted guinea hen with foie gras sauce and whiffs of unfounded culpability. Friday: mushrooms with garlic and patents.

Critical chaos. Viscous vertigo. Impressed by the aesthetic sublimation of gluttony. Uncommon thrill, overpowering pleasure in words made flesh. Transformed sight advances the incorrigible divisionist.

Herman Melville

Of all the heroes of anorexic activism, his Bartleby is without doubt the bravest and most unique. Converting lack of appetite into an act of resistance, he gradually unyoked from his bodily shell to fade away without leaving a trace, except for some ginger cookie crumbs that took the place of meals. In the blink of an eye or the quivering of a lip, notice the ghost of the uncooperative scribe. With what indifference will the shade testify against his own wasted flesh? There is so much noise and so much silence, so much freedom among such powerlessness. He refuses to refuse. In that, superior to other *Hungerkünstler*. Finally extinguished, but not before greeting a few anointed pitying faces.

James Joyce

On the menu: bread sticks wrapped with San Daniele prosciutto, goose salami, risotto with asparagus and walnut cakes. Looks at the tablecloth dirtied by previous patrons. Reads the local newspaper while shitting. Then wipes his ass with the day's news. To think excrement reanimates through excretion. Falls for a cute bourgeois woman who he could have seduced if he hadn't failed at his career as a neo-Renaissance guitar hero.

Today, melancholic tunes of Dowland can no longer console. A head totters over a blank page, and phrases escape, gather in irregular clusters. Recycling and converting epiphanies is a very weighty task, which falls to the artist kept awake by an awareness of finitude. And claim the purest, most perfect indifference, which is born of a word that gathers and honors the multitude of its own echoes.

Joris-Karl Huysmans

He will have to live on a piece of bread, potatoes and some fruit. To prepare meager and varied dinners, to overcome indifference and nausea. To eat the wrong way by means of complicated peptic purgatives, to discover in rotting corpses alkaline aromas capable of broadening the practices of cook, baker, confectioner in the domain of memory, reverence, contemplation and prayer. To get drunk with the fury of lost perfumes. To couple living and dead. Immortality in gaseous state.

Joseph Cornell

Less akin to Duchamp than Braque to Picasso. A bit more subtle, a bit more meticulous, but also a bit wiser and a bit more manageable. Divine indefatigable bargain hunter, his work knows no hiatus. They say he roasted his boxes in a low oven to make them look older and to cause them to split and crack. Nature also produces fakes (Charles Simic).

Marcel Broodthaers

The pot of mussels exists only via its equivalent volume. It reduces air's transparency, absorbs museum light. Some overrun this meeting with an annoying memory. Back home they eventually fall asleep, then wake up with a start as they exit terrible nightmares. Here's what clamors at us. The work would require a private, close reading. Touch would return to venture into an unlikely space where structure replaces form, presentation for the unpresentable, outside any yearning for knowledge.

A silhouette appears that glides in slow sweeps to the edge of the aquarium. The girl forgot about her accompanying family, tapping the vast walls, trying to attract the animal's attention, bothering its veils and diaphanous tentacles. The folds of this creature devoid of spine and mind suggest a world of poisonous caresses, healed wounds, welts, masks of grief and pity. Claimed to be inedible in our lands, it is appreciated by dolphins and turtles and eaten dried and salted in China, Japan, even Malaysia. The sensate gather and disperse around the umbrella that contracts gently, redeploys, swells, quivers, then tapers as it rises, driven by some mysterious decision. The jellyfish is nothing but body.

Marcel Duchamp

A thermometer and a cuttlefish bone with nothing in the mix from Montale. A cage filled with cubes stamped MADE IN FRANCE. Mannerisms in the absence of style. One day or another, the nominal sentence will eventually outskin ambient minimalism. *This makes it art.* The readymade neither deceives nor cheats. To the touch, the material remains constant. The strength of objects answers a new classicism, patient and monochrome. Then comes the opposite feat. Sugar hardens into diced metamorphic rocks' varicose faces. How many angels on the head of a pin? Speculation prevails through a kind of anorexic euphoria. The most stubborn among us will imagine the plumage of the absent bird.

Marcel Proust

One day I will knock on his door. For now, a whirl of mundane musings prevent me. I try to break loose, raise my head toward heaven and survey the creamy clouds. Barefoot on damp grass, I feel air expanded by heat become lighter. Suddenly rustling in trees surrounding me makes me shift my gaze and direct it toward an old bench upon which sits a young woman with brown hair, a blank look and long yellow dress. I pretend not to take notice of her, and she casts her eyes again toward the ground, I believe to discern, mixed with dust, some shred of affinity with the universe. I feel my face transform in a strange way while the city itself moves in a vacuum, stretches out, becomes every minute a little thinner. Colors are deep and dirty. Even deeper and dirtier. You could not tell if it's done with glue, with rubies, with soap, with bronze, with sun, with crap!

Asolo, 1979. There are ants in the hollow of the apricot tree and in the fissures of fallen fruit. Scent of pureed strawberry, stuffed buns and breaded zucchini blossoms. Then, the sound of footsteps retreat from the chicken coop with a peppery odor, where you carefully avoid stepping on fresh droppings. Plane trees and young vines line the paths of Biordo Vecchio hounded by the barking of a chained dog, partially masked by a moped's insistent drone. The animal is sick and old, you pass it by and don't notice a thing. In the morning's heat, the fragrance of jasmine, magnolia and lavender floating in the shadow of the church tower already belong to another world. I balance a beetle on a chestnut leaf. I observe and correct its hesitations and struggles, then deposit it in a row of roses before returning to my room. Years later, I find myself in another room, colder and where an appalling neatness reigns. And I (forgive me if I) attempt to piece together fragments of those old faded postcards that I had stashed a long time ago in the back of a drawer. For something or someone who continues to exist.

Max Ernst

In the west a new crescent moon. To the left, a dark and narrow building. Four lit doors. A padlock and a rusty length of chain prevent access to the building. But we must take refuge before the trail disappears permanently in darkness. Before everything eventually merges: hard, soft, bitter and sweet, noise and silence, pale and flushed, living and dead. Under an ambulance's flashing lights, the dreaded time of the wrench of bereavement arrived. This scene we read and reread in our youth.

Michel de Montaigne

Rome, 1580. Having completed his trip to Italy, and after having lodged two nights at the Locanda dell'Orso, where Rabelais stayed forty years before, he settled into rented rooms facing the church of Santa Lucia della Tinta. Looking out the window, filled with evening light that bathes the warm and smooth walls of the church, he wondered about what meaning war and the desire for conquest could well have at such a moment. Hamlet the pacifist will read those judgments and recite his own. *Even for an eggshell.*

Come evening, he loves putting fingers in the dish and is annoyed by the new set of protocols adopted by his contemporaries. In all likelihood, he ignores all of the different flavors of potato since the latter had just been introduced in Spain before winning over the rest of Europe. He does not know how to cook and barely tolerates Italian food, seasoned with oil, vinegar and salt, preferring drawn-out Germanic feasts with meats in sauce, more often than not accompanied by fruits, their bread fragrant with fennel, their white cabbages and clear white wines served in abundance.

Paul Claudel

Familiarity with rice. The artist invents shapeless and silent places. Sees the fossilized nests of swallows encrusted with granite. Weighted down by the last winds that whip idly through poplars. Ponge praises his sense of «imitative harmony.» How can you think about time when it clumps like peat?

Everything about the pig is good. A solitary and determined eater. Tolerates no table-companions and no one knows if it chews or drinks the disgusting slop it snarfs. It makes its way through the countryside like the farmer trudges through misty rice paddies.

Percy Bysshe Shelley

The disciple of John Frank Newton drags himself out of the tall grass, makes his way through a hole in the fence and returns to his garden. It is claimed that he dines almost exclusively on fruits and berries, picked at random on his walks. He nibbles them like a rodent. All this is greatly exaggerated because he also sings the praises of bread, green beans (not Pythagoras's gaseous beans), potatoes, peas, turnips, lettuce and, at least during winter, apples, oranges and pears.

Peter Greenaway

Soon vegetables are cooked in water and salt, without
   additional seasoning.
Soon guests spattering big gobs of red and milky spittle.
Soon an excellent observer of the waverings of common
   behaviors.
Soon reassured by the most rigid order.
Soon a chef famous for his black dishes.
Soon devouring death with great relish.
Soon baffled by horny boars and the metaphysics of
   flesh.
Soon will think no more about it.
Soon will think no more.
Soon drunkard stupified by sharp fumes of Jack
   Daniel's.
Soon entering a room where sausage links look like
   wet braids.
Soon visiting a holiday carnival in search of hot
   and sticky food.
Soon duck *à l'orange* and ham with pineapple.
Soon interspersed between courses of stuffed chicken,
   duck breast with bell peppers and blue trout.
Soon will be one.
Soon installed in the office to clip feathers.
Soon *joy of a toy* and *popsicle fun*.
Soon plainsong, without accidents, polyphonies or
   unnecessary solos.
Soon will announce the goals of his future
   profession.

Soon young charismatic preacher concocting a strange plan.
Soon will return home and will disengage simultaneously the smell of birth and old age.

Piero Manzoni

Expelling without effort or second thought, he surveys what's around him, hesitates, steps back, then freezes, immersed in a delight he had not experienced in a long time. Shit: the word is weak and abstract compared to those that preceded it in the agglutinative and alliterative language of infancy. Pee-pee, ca-ca, poo-poo: that's what makes the substance joyful. Piero, impressed by the array, opts for a serious word, lewd, tasteless. Worse yet, instead of observing and meditating on the indistinct, he decides to impose himself once and for all upon a flattened terrain, as if to trap throes of putrefaction, giving them more defined contours to better outlast them.

So far, more than the world or what lies beyond the world, this is the word that scares, drains blood from cheeks and ties stomachs into knots. Serialism bombards thirsty minds with consensual variations and collective strengths. It orchestrates our efforts at consumption, aims for exhausting substance and meaning. The philosophical system is poor, the theoretical apparatus borders on stuntedness. It's necessary to seek out but things, to whisper their essence, to shield them temporarily from the wanton dream machine. And not to protest until the time's right.

Salvador Dalí

Shapes of faded scents flowing, dripping, fermenting and drying out. Disturbing richness of camembert and malleable watches. Mystical flatulence of string beans. Exhibitionism of essential and materialogical turbulence. Serve with a spoon, oily, hairy and gamey — a gastro-aesthetic frenzy. In order to end the Apollonian scruples of cowards and careful art, those obsessed with linearity. Write a serious poem about mascarpone without as far as claiming that God is a mountain cheese, and New York a Gothic roquefort. Read the future in camembert. Look at the belly starting to swell. Compare the insipidity of Verlaine with Dutch cheese. Stay overnight to enjoy unlikely colonic cocktails. Observe milk leap toward immortality.

Samuel Beckett

Child, Beckett, following the example of Molloy, collects stones to suck on. He acquires them as if they are little orphans, looks after them preciously, washes them, fondles them, polishes them. They are actually his friends and sometimes he decorates the trees in his garden with them. His jacket pockets, worn with rain and sweat, recalls the womb in which the author said he felt so cramped, from which he claimed to scream from the depths of his intrauterine lungs.

Once outside, things get complicated. The voice is no longer muffled, static that tickles your ear. The mouth is filled with mud. Silence is not forthcoming, and you still can perceive the annoying buzzing of a fly that zigzags between your eyes and the infinite. Moodiness grants chance to fate. All these concessions take place during a time of profound inspiration that carries little by little the western horizon as far as its breaking point.

Yet, what follows still waits for something it, too, awaits. Sunday, the roof joists in the attic were black. Because, in the sky, thousands of blue flies had appeared to him one morning. Because, now, if they knock on your door, for you, who are no longer there for anything or anyone.

Steve Reich

Sometimes.
Sometimes disappear into the beauty of things.
Sometimes touch down.
Sometimes begin to crack and scream.
Sometimes noisily roll your *r*'s.
Sometimes white horse.
Sometimes slowly trace your hand across a delicate face.
Sometimes disappear behind the curtains.
Sometimes put his clothes on again, embarrassed, looking down at the ground.
Sometimes all around.
Sometimes lying in the dark.
Sometimes willing to believe and follow.
Sometimes walk together.
Sometimes rise and fall.
Sometimes start looking toward the top right dot.
Sometimes pale and light.
Sometimes red and dense and heavy.
Sometimes something.
Sometimes nothing.
Sometimes distant.
Sometimes even more distant.
Sometimes dragging the night in the company of its peers.
Sometimes afraid of being surprised while walking.
Sometimes last a long time.
Sometimes last.

WAYNE THIEBAUD

Nothing is further from Warholian fetishism than these strange soft contraptions. What's granted us to see here is that notorious sickness of substance that blurs the distinction between synthetic and organic, animal and human, solid and fluid. Here, all food is necessarily and unconditionally despicable and ridiculous.

Around the Cake (1962) presents us with a cake plastered on the canvas surrounded by eight almost identical slices laid out on white plates. Magic of icing and edible paint. Captivated by the accident that differentiates almost identical elements of assembly-line pastry. Erosion of the original under the effect of time and multiple reproductions. Those who seek a point of irony in this work would lose their time and trouble in it.

William Faulkner

Here there are no children. No laughter, no tears. And I stagger among the light glancing off carafes and windows, exuding odors of honey, burnt coffee, pickle juice. Our conversation comes to an end inauspiciously.

WIM DELVOYE

The celibate machine proceeds with unfailing and unusual logic while the viewer pays last repects to its missing organs. The order of questions posed leads to the paradox of an intransigent imagination. These tubes, jars and enzyme pumps seem wonderfully suited to freeing us from fatigue, heartburn and stomach cramps. And it's the same expression that dissipates while contemplating these strange water clocks of saiety. Deprived of feeling, a mechanical cloaca is in sheer coincidence with itself. Model of self-reflexiveness, he claims to sweep aside idealistic fantasies and purge us from fatal feelings, hating every ideology, ghostifying verbal and edible material.

WYNDHAM LEWIS

His naked feast embodies the worst modern nightmare. He eats without appetite, simply content to devour delicacies and empty dishes. He punishes the glutton and decayed-tooth cravings in the name of a living art that would protect its creative energy and would escape syndication and mass sentimentalism. More than anything else, it is the oyster that is repulsed by its energy and viscous sexuality. *No free lunch*. And especially not cups, jams or tea. And she, with white and ample cosmopolitan boobs, indifferent to the sight of her failing sweetness, until night fully conceals them.

Notes

The title of this book in French, *Entre la poire et le fromage*, signifies in Francophone cultures the point in a dinner, between the pear (or fruit) and cheese courses, when one is so satiated and comfortable that no topic is off the table for discussion.

In the original French, the author quotes specific passages in English. Those passages are indicated in this translation by rendering them in italics. In «Don Van Vliet» the italics refer to a specific painting by the artist.

quale [kwä-lay]: *Eng.* n 1. A property (such as hardness) considered apart from things that have that property. 2. A property that is experienced as distinct from any source it may have in a physical object. *Ital.* pron.a. 1. Which, what. 2. Who. 3. Some. 4. As, just as.

www.ingramcontent.com/pod-product-compliance
Lightning Source LLC
Chambersburg PA
CBHW031215090426
42736CB00009B/925